Self-Love
JOURNAL

AF391446

this journal perfectly complements the

Self-Love
WORKBOOK

This journal belongs to

Dear reader,

Welcome to my self-love journal. As the author of this journal, I want to express my deepest gratitude for choosing to embark on this journey with me. I understand that the journey to self-love can be challenging, and sometimes it can feel overwhelming. However, I'm confident that together we can explore and discover what it means to love and accept ourselves unconditionally.

Goals: My intention for this journal is to create a space where you can reflect, explore, and nurture your relationship with yourself. Through the exercises, prompts, and tools I have provided, I hope that you can achieve the following goals:

- Develop a deeper understanding of yourself and your needs
- Cultivate a positive and compassionate relationship with yourself
- Release self-doubt, self-judgment, and negative self-talk
- Embrace your unique qualities and strengths
- Create healthy self-care habits that nourish your body, mind, and spirit

Before we begin, I want to express my gratitude for your courage and willingness to prioritize your well-being. Choosing to embark on a journey toward self-love is a powerful decision, and I commend you for taking this step toward a happier and more fulfilling life. I'm grateful to be a part of this journey with you and look forward to supporting you every step of the way.

"Self-love is the source of all other loves."
Pierre Corneille

3-D Scan of You

Before we begin exploring different aspects of self-love, let's take a moment to create a 3-D scan of you. This exercise will help you gain a deeper understanding of your physical, emotional, and spiritual self. It's important to remember that self-love encompasses all aspects of who you are, and this scan will help you identify areas of strength and areas for growth.

Physical Scan: Start by focusing on your physical self. Close your eyes and take a few deep breaths. Then, slowly scan your body from head to toe. Take note of any physical sensations or areas of tension. How do you feel physically at this moment? Write down your observations in the physical scan section of this page.

Emotional Scan: Now, shift your focus to your emotional self. Ask yourself, how am I feeling emotionally in this moment? What emotions am I experiencing? Take a few deep breaths and allow yourself to feel whatever emotions come up. Write down your observations in the emotional scan section of this page.

Spiritual Scan: Finally, let's focus on your spiritual self. This may encompass your beliefs, values, sense of purpose, and connection to something greater than yourself. Take a few deep breaths and ask yourself, what does spirituality mean to me? How do I connect with my spiritual self? Write down your observations in the spiritual scan section of this page.

Knowing myself better

Self Care Ideas

BASIC

PHYSICAL

EMOTIONAL

SPIRITUAL

FEEL READY FOR MY JOURNAL

Journaling

Write a love letter to yourself, as if you were your own secret admirer.

I am motivated.

I am productive.

I am successful.

I am honest.

Word association Game

Choose a word related to self-love, such as "**compassion**" or "**acceptance**," and write down as many words or phrases that come to mind when you think of that word.

I am charming.

What is the most bizarre dream you have ever had?

If you could swap lives with any cartoon character, whom would it be and why?

My Journey of Self-Discovery:

The Basic "Me" Part of My Journal

Explore and reflect upon the various aspects of yourself, such as your values, beliefs, strengths, weaknesses, and aspirations. By getting to know yourself better, you can cultivate a deeper sense of self-awareness and self-acceptance and discover new opportunities for personal growth and fulfillment.

A brief introduction to who I am, where I come from, and what makes me unique.

Reflections: What are some of the key experiences or events that have shaped me into the person I am today? What are some of the challenges, triumphs, and lessons that I have learned along the way?

An exploration of my core values and beliefs, and how they shape my perspective and actions.

Reflections: What are the values and beliefs that I hold dear, and why are they important to me? How do these values and beliefs influence my decision-making, relationships, and life goals?

An assessment of my strengths and weaknesses, and how they contribute to my personal and professional life.

____

____

____

____

____

____

____

Reflections: What are some of my greatest strengths and talents, and how can I leverage them to achieve my goals and make a positive impact on others? What are some of my weaknesses and areas for improvement, and how can I address them to become a better version of myself?

____

____

____

____

____

____

____

A vision for my future, and the goals and aspirations that I hope to achieve.

Reflections: What are some of the things that I want to accomplish or experience in my life, and why are they meant to me? How can I break down these dreams and aspirations into actionable steps and timelines, and make progress toward realizing them?

I am enough.

I choose happiness.

I deserve love.

I am worthy.

Acrostic poems Game

Write a word related to self-love vertically down the page, and use each letter as the first letter of a word or phrase that describes what self-love means to you.

I am capable.

Draw a portrait of yourself as a famous historical figure who practiced self-love.

I am confident.

I am grateful.

What are some things that you need to forgive yourself for, and
how can you work towards self-compassion and acceptance?

I am strong.

I am loved.

I am beautiful.

If you could switch lives with any fictional character for a day, whom would it be and why?

If you had a talking pet that gave you self-love advice, what kind of animal would it be and what would it say to you?

My Journey of Self-Discovery:

The Physical Me Part of My Journal

Explore and reflect upon your physical health, appearance, and well-being. By paying attention to your body, you may develop a greater appreciation and care for yourself, and make positive changes that support your overall health and happiness.

An exploration of my relationship with my body, and how it affects my self-esteem and self-worth.

Reflections: How do I feel about my physical appearance and body image? What are some of the negative or positive thoughts and emotions that come up when I think about my body? How can I develop a more positive and loving relationship with my body, and cultivate a stronger sense of self-esteem and self-acceptance?

An assessment of my current physical health and wellness, and how I can improve it.

____

____

____

____

____

____

____

Reflections: What are some of the habits and behaviors that contribute to my physical health, such as nutrition, exercise, sleep, and stress management? How can I incorporate more healthy and nourishing practices into my daily routine, and create a sustainable and balanced lifestyle that supports my well-being?

____

____

____

____

____

____

____

An exploration of how I can take care of myself physically and emotionally, and promote relaxation and stress relief.

Reflections: What are some of the self-care practices that I enjoy, such as taking a bath, getting a massage, or practicing meditation? How can I incorporate more of these activities into my life, and make self-care a priority? What are some of how I can relax and unwind, and reduce the effects of stress on my body and mind?

A reflection on my personal style and how it reflects my identity and personality.

Reflections: What are some of the fashion and beauty choices that I make, and how do they express my individuality and creativity? How can I experiment with new styles and looks, and step outside of my comfort zone? How can I embrace and celebrate my unique physical attributes and qualities?

I am deserving.

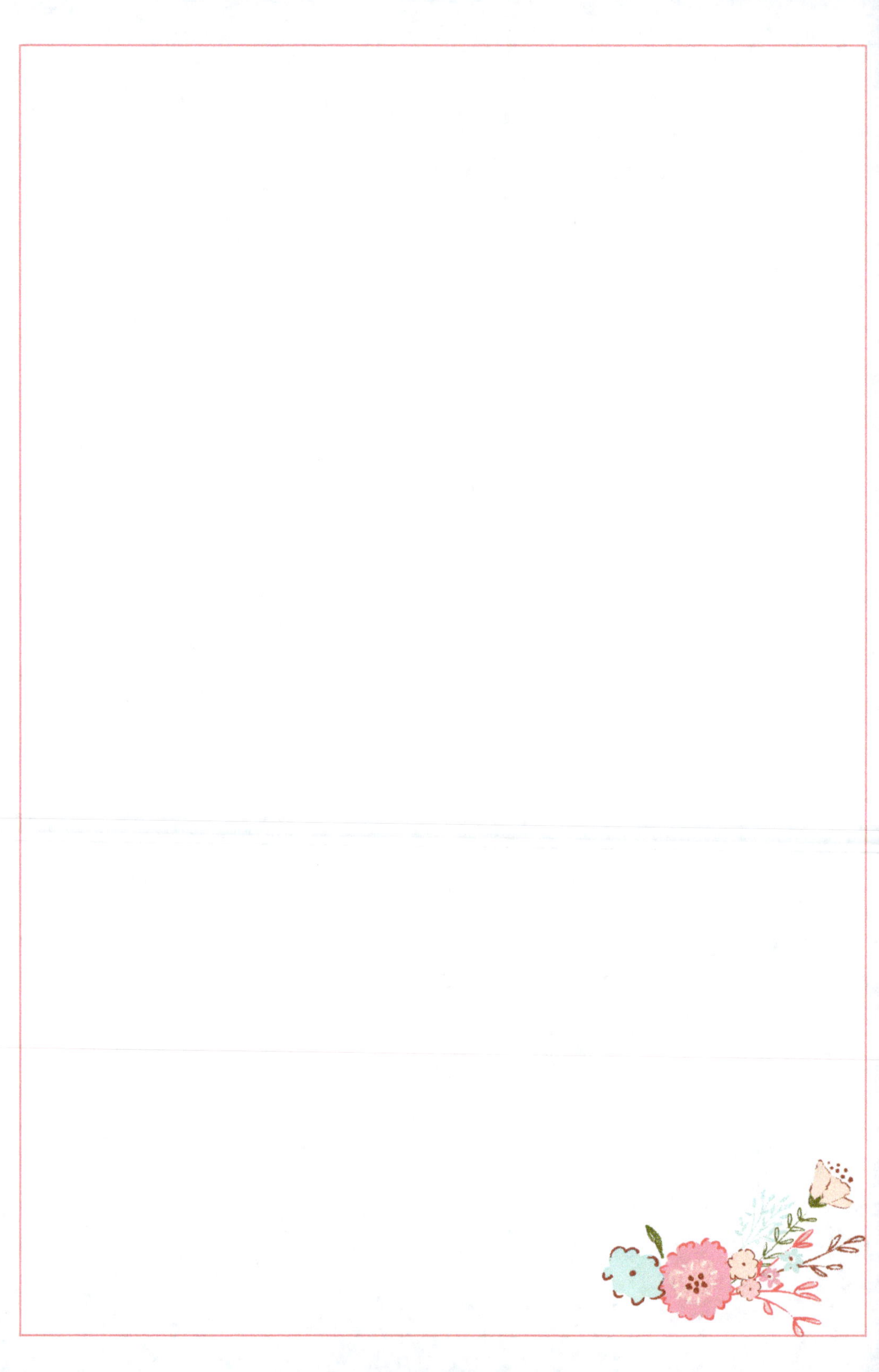

I am valuable.

I am unique.

I am special.

Anagrams Game

- Rearrange the letters of the words below to create as many new words as possible.
- Each word must be at least 3 letters long.
- Proper nouns, hyphenated words, and abbreviations are not allowed.

mindfulness

forgiveness

happiness

I am important.

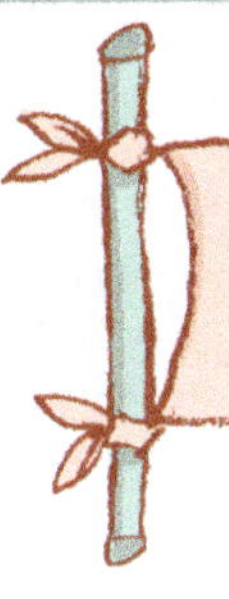

Write a recipe for your favorite comfort food and add a self-love ingredient to it.

I am respected.

I am kind.

I am patient.

I am understanding.

What are some things that make you happy, and how can you
incorporate more of them into your daily life?

I am generous.

If you could have any superpower, what would it be and how would you use it to boost your self-love?

Imagine you could only communicate through interpretive dance for a day - what kind of dance moves would you show to express your self-love?

My Journey of Self-Discovery:

The Emotional Me Part of My Journal

Explore and reflect upon your emotions, thoughts, and feelings. By paying attention to your inner world, you may develop a greater understanding and acceptance of yourself, and cultivate a more compassionate and authentic relationship with your emotions.

An exploration of my emotional landscape, and how I express and communicate my feelings.

Reflections: How aware am I of my emotions, and how do I process and express them? What are some of the ways in which I communicate my feelings, such as through journaling, art, or talking with others? How can I develop a more nuanced and healthy relationship with my emotions, and cultivate more self-awareness and emotional intelligence?

A reflection on how I cope with difficult emotions, such as sadness, anger, or anxiety.

Reflections: What are some of the difficult emotions that I struggle with, and how do they affect me? What are some of the coping mechanisms that I use, such as distraction, avoidance, or numbing? How can I develop more effective and healthy strategies for dealing with difficult emotions, such as mindfulness, self-compassion, or seeking support?

An exploration of my relationships with others, and how they impact my emotional well-being.

Reflections: What are some of the important relationships in my life, and how do they contribute to my emotional landscape? What are some of the ways in which I connect with others, such as through intimacy, vulnerability, or empathy? How can I develop more fulfilling and meaningful relationships, and cultivate more intimacy and authenticity with others?

A reflection on the positive emotions that I experience, such as gratitude and joy.

Reflections: What are some of the things that bring me joy and happiness, and how can I cultivate more of these experiences in my life? What are some of the people, events, or moments that I am grateful for, and how do they contribute to my sense of well-being and fulfillment? How can I practice gratitude and joy as a way of cultivating a more positive and resilient emotional landscape?

I am authentic.

"Fantasy Day"

Imagine your dream day, filled with activities and experiences that bring you joy and fulfillment. Write down every detail, from what you wear to what you eat to whom you spend time with.

I am creative.

I am inspired.

I am blessed.

I am passionate.

What are some qualities that you look for in a supportive friend or partner, and how can you cultivate those qualities within yourself?

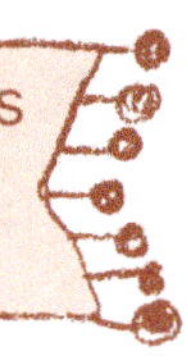

Take a picture of yourself making a ridiculous face and write a positive affirmation about self-love next to it.

____

____

____

____

I am radiant.

I am graceful.

"Compliment Blitz"

Write down as many positive things about yourself as you can think of in five minutes. Don't censor yourself or worry about being too boastful – just let the self-love flow!

I am flexible.

I am balanced.

What are some negative experiences or traumas that you've faced,
and how can you use self-love and self-care to heal from them?

I am calm.

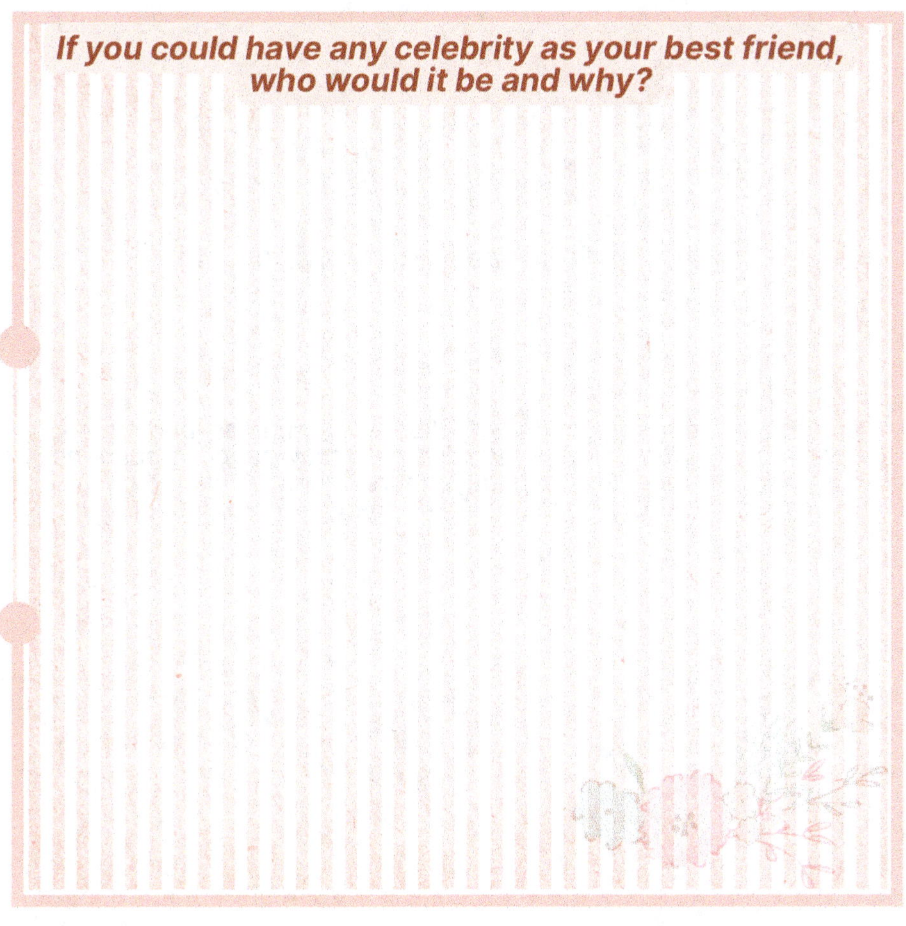

If you could have any celebrity as your best friend, who would it be and why?

If you could only wear one outfit for the rest of your life, what would it be and why?

My Journey of Self-Discovery:
The Spiritual Me Part of My Journal

Explore and reflect upon your spiritual beliefs, practices, and experiences. By connecting with your inner wisdom, you may deepen your sense of purpose and meaning, and cultivate a more authentic and compassionate relationship with yourself and the world around you.

A reflection on my spiritual beliefs and values, and how they shape my worldview.

Reflections: What are some of my core spiritual beliefs, such as the nature of reality, the purpose of life, or the existence of a higher power? How do these beliefs inform my values and priorities, such as compassion, kindness, or service? How can I deepen my understanding and connection with my spiritual beliefs, and cultivate a more integrated and holistic sense of self?

An exploration of my spiritual practices and rituals, and how they support my well-being and growth.

Reflections: What are some of the spiritual practices that I engage in, such as meditation, prayer, or yoga? How do these practices help me connect with my inner wisdom, and cultivate a greater sense of peace and presence? What are some of the rituals that I find meaningful and nourishing, such as lighting candles, reading spiritual texts, or communing with nature? How can I deepen my spiritual practice, and integrate it more fully into my daily life?

A reflection on the spiritual qualities of gratitude and surrender, and how they support my growth and transformation.

Reflections: What does gratitude mean to me, and how do I practice it in my daily life? How does cultivating an attitude of gratitude help me connect with my inner wisdom, and appreciate the beauty and abundance of life? What does surrender mean to me, and how do I practice it in moments of challenge or uncertainty? How can I cultivate a deeper sense of trust and surrender in my spiritual journey, and let go of attachments and expectations?

An exploration of the spiritual qualities of service and connection, and how they support my sense of purpose and meaning.

Reflections: What does service mean to me, and how do I engage in acts of kindness and generosity? How does serving others help me connect with my inner wisdom, and cultivate a greater sense of purpose and meaning? What does connection mean to me, and how do I foster deeper connections with myself and others? How can I cultivate more meaningful and authentic relationships, and contribute to the greater good of humanity?

I am peaceful.

I am serene.

I am confident.

"Mood Boosters"

Create a list of things that instantly improve your mood, such as listening to a favorite song, dancing, or snuggling with a pet. Refer to this list whenever you need a pick-me-up

What are some fears or limiting beliefs that are holding you back, and how can you work towards overcoming them with self-love and self-acceptance?

I am unstoppable.

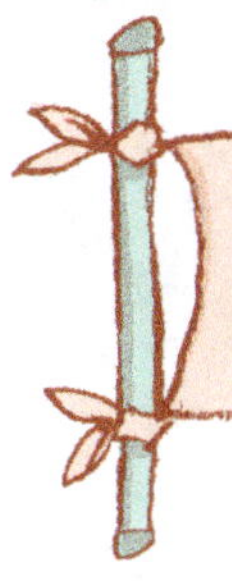

Write a list of all the silly things you do that make you happy and show yourself some self-love.

Create a playlist of empowering songs that make you feel like a self-love warrior.

I am fearless.

I am resilient.

I am invincible.

What are some ways that you can cultivate a deeper sense of gratitude and appreciation for yourself, your life, and the people and experiences around you?

I am respected.

I am intelligent.

Write a short story where you're the main character and you have to rescue yourself with self-love.

I am open-minded.

I am me. I love me. I deserve me.

*If you could have any celebrity as your best friend,
whom would it be and why?*

If you could only wear one outfit for the rest of your life,
what would it be and why?

"Self-Portrait"

Draw or paint a picture of yourself, capturing your unique features and personality. Don't worry about making it perfect – just have fun and celebrate your individuality.